Spanish Verb Tenses

How to Conjugate Spanish Verbs,
Perfecting Your Mastery of Spanish Verbs in all the
Tenses and Moods

Brandon Simpson

Small Town Press
Dry Ridge, KY

D1342306

ACKNOWLEDGEMENTS

I would like to thank all my Spanish instructors I've ever had. I would also like to thank all my Spanish-speaking friends.

ISBN: 978-0-9816466-2-6

www.BrandonSimpson.net

About the Author

Brandon Simpson has a Bachelor of Arts degree in Spanish. In addition to Spanish, he minored in French and has also studied other languages as a hobby. He is the author of *Demystifying Spanish Grammar*.

Read more about him at www.BrandonSimpson.net

DISCLAIMER

Neither the author nor the publisher can be held liable for the misuse of this book. The explanations herein are merely here to help your comprehension of Spanish grammar. Every possible effort was taken to ensure the accuracy of the information in this book. There may be, however, mistakes that neither the author nor the editors noticed. Some of the information in this book was provided by native speakers who are not necessarily experts of grammar. Reading this book will not guarantee mastery of the material nor will it guarantee a higher grade. This book is not endorsed by any company mentioned. The reader also acknowledges that this book is not comprehensive. Readers should, and are also encouraged, to seek the advice of competent individuals.

Spanish Verb Tenses:
How to Conjugate Spanish Verbs,
Perfecting Your Mastery of Spanish Verbs in all
the Tenses and Moods

Table of Contents

1 Introduction

Learning how to properly use the verb tenses in Spanish is no easy task. It will take a lot of time and work to master them. In this book are detailed explanations of the present tenses, past tenses, future tenses, conditional tenses, the subjunctive, and more.

Before we get started with the tenses, you need to know the subject pronouns in Spanish. They are:

yo	I	nosotros (as)	we
tú	you (inf. sing.)	vosotros (as)	you-all (inf)
usted	you (for. sing.)	ustedes	you-all (for)
él	he	ellos	they (m or m/f)
ella	she	ellas	they (all f)

As you can see, there are four ways of saying *you* in Spanish. *Tú* is used for friends, family, pets, and God. *Usted* is used for people you don't know or anyone who is older than you. In Latin America, *ustedes* is used as both the informal and formal way of saying *you-all*. In Spain, however, the pronoun *vosotros* is used as the informal plural.

Latin America

tú + tú	ustedes
tú + usted	ustedes
usted + usted	ustedes

Spain

tú + tú	vosotros (as)
tú + usted	ustedes
usted +	ustedes
usted	

Person and Number

The words *person* and *number* will be used throughout this book. So we should learn what they mean now. *Number* deals with whether or not the pronoun is singular or plural. The definition of *person* is hard to understand. Anything or anyone in the 3rd person is being talked *about*. Anyone is the 2nd person is being spoken *to*. And the 1st person is the one who is speaking. Look at the following chart of subject pronouns in English.

Subject Pronouns

Person	Singular	Plural
1	I	we
2	you	you
3	he/she/it	they

2 Present Tenses

Usage

The present tense in Spanish is used for four situations: **SAFE**.

Simple Facts
Actions in Progress
Future Actions
Emphatic Present

Formation

Forming the present tense is easier said than done. We must first determine what verb we are conjugating. Spanish verbs can be divided into two large groups: regular and irregular. Regular verbs are verbs that follow a pattern. Irregular verbs do not follow any pattern. Many Spanish grammar books list some verbs as irregular, but they really aren't. They simply follow a different pattern. Look at the following figure.

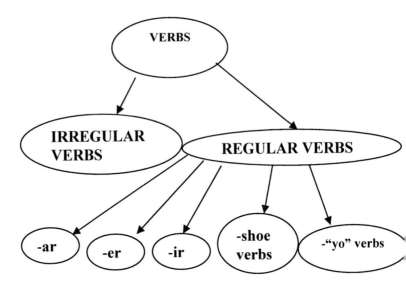

As you can see, verbs can be divided into two large groups: irregular and regular. The regular verbs can be divided into five sub-groups. First, we'll learn how to conjugate the regular verbs.

Regular Verbs

-ar verbs are those verbs whose infinitive ends in – ar. The most commonly used example of an –ar verb is *hablar*. Here's how to conjugate an –ar verb:

1. Take the infinitive. (hablar)
2. Remove the ending. (habl-)
3. Add the appropriate personal endings to the stem. (Endings are italicized in the following table)

hablar – to speak

habl*o*	habl*amos*
habl*as*	habl*ais*
habl*a*	habl*an*

-er verbs are those verbs whose infinitive ends in – er. To conjugate an –er verb, we follow the same steps we did when conjugated an –ar verb, except the *a* gets replaced with an *e*.

comer – to eat

com*o*	com*emos*
com*es*	com*eis*
com*e*	com*en*

-ir verbs resemble –er verbs, but the *nosotros* and *vosotros* forms of –ir verbs differ from that of –er verbs. Look at the chart below.

vivir – to eat

viv*o*	viv*imos*
viv*es*	viv*ís*
viv*e*	viv*en*

All regular verbs follow the pattern of these three verbs.

Shoe Verbs

Shoe verbs are verbs whose stem has a vowel change. Many teachers classify these as irregular verbs, but I disagree. If there is a predictable pattern, it is regular. Being classified as a regular verb will help you to remember them better as well.

To learn the concept of "shoe verbs," we'll use the verbs *jugar, mostrar, pensar, poder, querer, pedir, vestir,* and *preferir.* In the following charts, imagine that the bolded verb forms are in a shoe.

jugar-to play (u-ue)

juego	jugamos
juegas	jugáis
juega	**juegan**

*As far as I know, this is the only *u-ue* shoe verb.

mostrar-to show (o-ue)

muestro	mostramos
muestras	mostráis
muestra	**muestran**

pensar-to think (e-ie)

pienso	pensamos
piensas	pensáis
piensa	**piensan**

poder-to be able, can (o-ue)

puedo	podemos
puedes	podéis
puede	**pueden**

querer-to want (e-ie)

quiero	queremos
quieres	queréis
quiere	**quieren**

pedir-to ask for, to order (e-i)

pido	pedimos
pides	pedís
pide	piden

vestir-to dress (e-i)

visto	vestimos
vistes	vestís
viste	visten

preferir-to prefer (e-ie)

prefiero	preferimos
prefieres	preferís
prefiere	prefieren

As you can tell from these examples, the endings are completely regular. It is only the stem that actually changes.

Another question I hear is *How do you tell when a verb has a stem change?* The answer to this is complicated. It is better to consult a dictionary or a verb book. But I'll try to give you a good explanation.

If the verb's stem vowel is *o* or *e*, there is a good possibility that there is a stem change. We'll use *poder* as our example. The verb *poder* is pronounced [po-ˈdɛɾ]. The last syllable is stressed. (The last syllable of all infinitives is stressed). When *poder* is conjugated in the *yo* form, it would become *podo* if it were completely regular. But now the tonic stress has changed. Now the first *o* is receiving the tonic stress. But in this case, the *o* can't receive the tonic stress. It is under so much "stress" that it has to become a diphthong, i.e. *ue*.

Remember that this is a very general rule. The verb *comer* would also be a shoe verb if this were an actual rule. To understand the actual rule behind this, you would have to know some Latin.

Another question that many Spanish students have regards the *e-ie* and *e-i* verbs. How do you know when to change the *e* to *ie* or to *i*? Luckily, there aren't many *e-i* verbs. The most common verbs of this type are *pedir* and *vestir*. From what I've noticed, only –ir verbs have *e-i* stem-changing verbs.

Another question you may have is *Which vowel changes if there are two?* If you ever see such a verb, the vowel that changes is *always* the second-to-last vowel of the infinitive. Here's an example:

preferir-to prefer (e-ie)

prefiero	preferimos
prefieres	preferís
prefiere	**prefieren**

There are two *es*, but only one can change. To my knowledge, *preferir* is the only stem-changing verb that has two similar vowels. But there are probably more.

Special "yo" Forms

There are several verbs that are completely regular, but they have a special *yo* form. These are often listed as irregular. Usually, the verb has a special *yo* form due to a spelling convention. Sometimes, however, the special *yo* from has no rhyme or reason. Look at the following examples:

escoger-to choose

escojo	escogemos
escoges	escogéis
escoge	escogen

eligir-to elect

elijo	eligimos
elijges	eligís
elige	eligen

This verb has a special *yo* to preserve the [h] sound ([x] in most dialects). If it were spelled with a *g*, it would be pronounced [es-ko-go] instead of the correct [es-ko-ho] or [es-ko-xo].

traducir-to translate

traduzco	traducimos
traduces	traducís
traduce	traducen

conducir-to drive

conduzco	conducimos
conduces	conducís
conduce	conducen

These two verbs follow the same "special *yo* form" pattern. As you can see, the special *yo* forms in these two verbs don't make any sense.

saber-to know

sé	sabemos
sabes	sabéis
sabe	saben

dar-to give

doy	damos
das	dais
da	dan

The special *yo* form for *saber* and *dar* have no rhyme or reason.

More examples:

caber-to fit

quepo	cabemos
cabes	cabéis
cabe	caben

caer-to fall, to drop

caigo	cameos
caes	caéis
cae	caen

coger-to seize, to take hold of

cojo	cogemos
coges	cogéis
coge	cogen

hacer-to do, to make

hago	hacemos
haces	hacéis
hace	hacen

nacer-to be born, to give birth

nazco	nacemos
naces	nacéis
nace	nacen

parecer-to appear

parezco	paracemos
pareces	paracéis
parece	paracen

poner-to put, to place

pongo	ponemos
pones	ponies
pone	ponen

traer-to bring

traigo	traemos
traes	traéis
trae	traen

Hybrids

More than likely, when you study verbs like *tener* and *venir*, you'll be told that they are completely irregular. But you can easily say that they are regular. When a verb has both a stem-change and a special *yo* form, I call it a *hybrid*. I find it easier to remember them like this.

tener-to have

tengo	tenemos
tienes	tenéis
tiene	tienen

venir-to come

vengo	venimos
vienes	venís
viene	vienen

The verbs *tener* and *venir* both follow the *e-ie* stem change. But they also have a special *yo* form.

Another example:

decir-to tell, to say (*e-i* with special *yo* form)

digo	decimos
dices	decís
dice	dicen

Completely Irregular Verbs

Now that we've examined the regular verbs, we can move on to the irregular verbs. These are the verbs that follow no logical pattern. Their forms must be memorized by heart. These are usually learned first in Spanish classes. They are the most commonly used verbs, which is why they are irregular. In this section we'll look at *ser, estar, ir,* and *haber.*

ser-to be

soy	somos
eres	sois
es	son

estar-to be

estoy	estamos
estás	estáis
está	están

ir- to go

voy	vamos
vas	vais
va	van

haber- to have

he	hemos
has	habéis
ha	han

As you can see, these four verbs follow no logical pattern at all. They must be memorized.

Verbs Like "gustar"

The verb *gustar* is regular, but its construction is different from that of other verbs. Look at the following example:

Me gusta este carro.
I like this car.

You may think that *me* means *I* in this sentence, but it does not. You see, *gustar* does not actually mean *to like*. It means *to please*. And the subject of this verb doesn't precede it; it follows it. So *Me gusta este carro* actually means *This car pleases me*.

To learn how these verbs work, you will need to know the indirect object pronouns.

me	nos
te	os
le	les

Other verbs that follow the same pattern as *gustar* include, but are not limited to, the following: *encantar, doler, interesar,* and *fascinar*.

Most Spanish students assume that anything that follows *gustar* is its direct object. But we've already established that the subject follows it. So the verb must also agree in number.

Examples:

Me gusta este carro.
I like this car.
(This car pleases me.)

Me gustan estos carros.
I like these cars.
(These cars please me.)

Me interesa la astronomía.
I'm interested in astronomy.
(Astronomy is interesting to me.)

Me interesan la astronomía y la química.
I'm interested in astronomy and chemistry.
(Astronomy and chemistry are interesting to me.)

Reflexive Verbs

In Spanish you'll see many infinitives that end in *–se*. These are called reflexive verbs. The subject of the verb is also its direct object. Look at the following sentences:

Yo lavo el carro.
I'm washing the car.

Lavo is the verb. The subject is *yo*, and its direct object is *el carro.*

Yo me lavo.
I'm washing myself.

Again, *lavo* is the verb. The subject is *yo*, but the direct object is *me*. The subject is performing the action on itself. In other words, the action is being *reflected* back on the subject. To learn reflexive verbs, you'll need to know the reflexive pronouns:

me	nos
te	os
se	se

llamarse- to call oneself

me llamo	nos llamamos
te llamas	os llamáis
se llama	se llaman

vestirse- to dress oneself

me visto	nos vestimos
te vistes	os vestís
se viste	se visten

The meaning is not always reflexive when you see *se* or another reflexive pronoun. Sometimes, the meaning is reciprocal. Look at the following sentence:

Los niños se miran.
The children are looking at each other.

The pronoun *se* can be used for the following situations:

1. Reflexive meaning – Action reflects back to the subject
2. Reciprocal – This translates to *each other*. It's only possible when the verb is plural.
3. No-fault construction – (More on this later)
4. Alternative to the Passive voice

The reflexive verb *irse* doesn't have reflexive or reciprocal meaning. When no destination is implied, you use *irse* instead of *ir*.

irse-to go away

me voy	nos vamos
te vas	os vais
se va	se van

Present Progressive

Just like English, Spanish has a present progressive tense. In English it is formed with the verb *to be* and the present participle (the *–ing* form). In Spanish it is formed with the verb *estar* plus the present participle.

The Spanish present participle is formed by removing the infinitive ending and adding the appropriate participle ending.

hablar – hablando
comer – comiendo
vivir – viviendo

Example:

Estoy hablando.
I am talking.

The use of the present progressive differs from the English present progressive slightly. It isn't used as much as it is in English. (However, I've noticed that several Spanish speakers in the

U.S. use it more that other Spanish speakers.) And it is only used to describe an action that is happening at the moment. In English it is often used to convey a future action. This is not possible in Spanish.

I'm taking a test on Monday.
(conveys future action)

Estoy haciendo un examen el lunes.
(not correct)

Hago un examen el lunes.
(correct: the present tense can be used to convey a future action)

Voy a hacer un examen el lunes.
I'm going to take a test on Monday.
(Future construction with *ir* can also be used)

Expressing the Future with "ir"

The Spanish verb *ir* can be used to express actions that occur in the future. It is formed by conjugating *ir* in the present tense, adding the preposition *a* and the infinitive of the main verb. I have heard this called the *fake future* and the *compound future/futuro compuesto*. Most books simply call it *ir+a+INFINITIVE*.

Example:

Voy a comer a las cinco.
I'm going to eat at 5.

You may wonder why it is necessary to add the *a* when the word *to* is already implied in the verb. The Spanish verb *ir* is always followed by *a*, *para*, or some other preposition. (This is excluding the verb *irse*.) The compound future is the preferred way of expressing future actions in Spanish. A future tense in Spanish does exist, but its use as a way to express the future isn't as common. More on that later.

Tricky Verbs

When learning Spanish, you'll learn that one verb in English can have two or more counterparts in Spanish. But there is almost always a logical reason why. Let's start with the *to be* verbs.

There are five Spanish verbs that can mean *to be*. The most common two are *ser* and *estar*, which actually translate directly to the verb *to be*. Many teachers and grammar books tell you that *ser* is permanent and that *estar* is temporary. But this explanation is extremely flawed. When I teach these two verbs, I use the acronyms **JETCO** and **LET**.

ser – JETCO

Jobs/Identification Statements
Event location
Telling time
Characteristics
Origin/nationality

estar- LET

Location (not event)
Emotions
Temporary feelings

These two verbs are explained more thoroughly in *Demystifying Spanish Grammar*.

Other verbs that can mean *to be* include *tener, hacer,* and *hay*. *Tener* literally means *to have, hacer* means *to do/to make,* and *hay* means *there is/there are*. The word *hay* is explained in chapter 8.

The following are idiomatic constructions that use *tener* as a *to be* verb.

tener _____ años – to be _____ years old
tener frío – to be cold
tener calor – to be hot
tener prisa – to be in a hurry
tener hambre – to be hungry

Hacer means *to be* when we use idiomatic expressions that deal with the weather.

Hace calor. – It is hot.
Hace frío. – It is cold.
Hace viento. – It is windy.
Hace sol. – It is sunny.

Now we'll examine three verbs that mean *to have*. You may wonder why there would be three in Spanish if we only need one in English. Well, the English verb *to have* can be used for the following:

1. Expressing possession.
   I have a car.
   Tengo un carro.

2. Expressing a past action.
   I have spoken.
   He hablado.

3. Expressing obligation.
   I have to go.
   Debo irme./Tengo que irme.

As you can see, the English verb *to have* can be *tener, haber,* or *deber.*

Another English verb that can have three different translations is the verb *to work.* In Spanish we have *trabajar, funcionar,* and *operar.* Which one do you use? Easy. *Trabajar* is used when you say you are doing actual labor, i.e.

Trabajo en un restaurant.
I work in a restaurant.

Funcionar is used when you are talking about a machine or a vehicle being in working condition, i.e.

Este carro no funciona.
This car doesn't work (function).

Operar is used when you are talking about operating something, i.e.

No sé operar esta máquina.
I don't know how to work (operate) this machine.

Making Questions

Making questions in Spanish is not difficult, but so many students are so used to how English has to use the verb *to do* to make questions that it becomes a little more difficult. In Spanish there is no need for a helping verb. Instead, Spanish makes questions in one of the three following ways:

1. Rising Intonation (voice rises at the end)
   ¿Tú hablas español?

2. Inversion (subject and verb are inverted)
   ¿Hablas tú español?

3. ¿No? (tag question)
   Tú hablas español, ¿no?

You must still raise the pitch of your voice at the end with each way of making questions.

Negation

Negating Spanish sentences is fairly easy compared to English. All you have to do is add the adverb *no* before the conjugated verb.

Example:
Ella habla español.
She speaks Spanish.

Ella no habla español.
She doesn't speak Spanish.

Other negative adverbs include the following:

nunca – never
no...ni...ni... - neither .... nor
nada – nothing
nadie – nobody
jamás – never

In English it is not correct to have double negatives, but it is required in Spanish.

Example:
No veo nada.
I don't see anything.

The "vos" Conjugation

Almost every book on Spanish grammar completely ignores the *vos* conjugation. Some even ignore the *vosotros* forms, which I don't agree with. If you've never heard of it, it is a second person singular pronoun used in many Latin American countries. It is used on a daily basis in Argentina in place of *tú*. It is also used in Chile, Uruguay, Nicaragua, and northern parts of Venezuela.

In order to learn the *vos* forms, you need to know the *vosotros* forms. Luckily, *vos* only has special forms in the present indicative, the present subjunctive, and in the imperative. The Argentine conjugation is probably the "standard" form of *vos*. To conjugate a verb in the *vos* form, take the *vosotros* form and eliminate the *i* (except for –ir verbs).

Examples:

vosotros habláis – vos hablás
vosotros coméis – vos comés
vosotros vivís – vos vivís

The conjugation of *vos* differs from country to country. In Chile, it is formed by taking the *vosotros* form and removing the *s*.

Examples:

vos hablái
vos coméi
vos viví

In other parts of Latin America, the pronoun *vos* can take the *tú* or *vosotros* forms.

Examples:

vos hablas/vos habláis
vos comes/vos coméis
vos vives/vos vivís

You may be wondering why this pronoun would even exist. In the beginning, Spanish only had two second person pronouns: *tú* and *vos*. *Tú* was used in the same as it is today. *Vos* was used as the second person plural pronoun and as the second person singular formal pronoun. It was like the distinction between *tu* and *vous* in French. When people spoke to someone more important than them, they used *Vuestra Merced (Your Lordship)*. This eventually became the pronoun *usted*. *Vosotros* was formed by adding *otros* to *vos*. Eventually, the pronoun *vos* was dropped except in certain countries and in Ladino.

3 Past Tenses

Now that we've learned the present tense and all its uses, we can move on to the past tenses. In this chapter you'll learn the imperfect, the preterit, the imperfect progressive, the preterit progressive, the immediate past, the *pluscuamperfecto*, the preterit perfect, and the present perfect. Conjugating these tenses isn't hard, but knowing when and how to use them is.

Imperfect

The imperfect is formed by taking the infinitive, removing the infinitive ending, and adding the appropriate ending.

hablar – to speak

hablaba	hablábamos
hablabas	hablabais
hablaba	hablaban

comer – to eat

comía	comíamos
comías	comíais
comía	comían

vivir – to live

vivía	vivíamos
vivías	vivíais
vivía	vivían

There are only three irregular verbs in the imperfect, but it could be said that they are regular. The stems are actually irregular. All three verbs have the same endings.

ser – to be

era	éramos
eras	erais
era	eran

ir – to go

iba	íbamos
ibas	ibais
iba	iban

ver – to see

veía	veíamos
veías	veíais
veía	veían

To learn the uses of the imperfect, use the acronym **HIDE**.

Habitual actions (used to + verb)
Incomplete actions (was/were + ing form of verb)
Descriptions in the past
Emotions/feelings

Whenever English uses the habitual past (used to + verb), Spanish uses the imperfect. This rule, however, has a few exceptions. Whenever English uses the past progressive (was/were + ing form of verb), Spanish ALWAYS uses the imperfect. The imperfect is also used to describe things in the past, and it is used when expressing one's emotions. Many Spanish grammar books say that the imperfect is used when something happens repeatedly, but this is a flawed explanation. If one said *Leí este libro*, it would require the preterit. According to the flawed explanation, you would have to say *Leía este libro dos veces* if you wanted to say *I read this book twice*. However, this is incorrect. It should be *Leí este libro dos veces*. When those grammar books say that the imperfect is used for actions that happen repeatedly, they mean to say that it is used for habitual actions (used to + verb).

Examples of imperfect:

Siempre iba al cine cuando yo era joven.
I always went to the movies when I was young.

Ella hablaba en francés.
She was speaking in French.

Su carro era blanco y solamente tenía tres llantas.
His car was white and only had three tires.

No me sentía bien.
I didn't feel well.

Preterit

Conjugating the preterit is more difficult because there are so many irregular verbs. But just like verbs in the present tense, these "irregular" verbs can usually be considered regular.

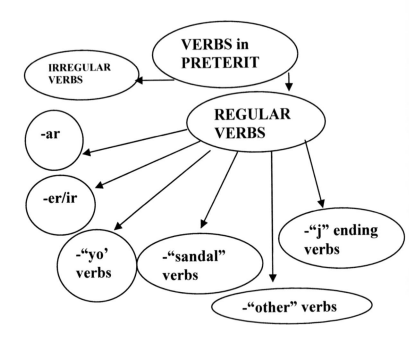

Regular Verbs in the Preterit

-ar verbs
hablar – to speak

hablé	hablamos
hablaste	hablasteis
habló	hablaron

-er verbs
comer – to eat

comí	comimos
comiste	comisteis
comió	comieron

-ir verbs
vivir – to live

viví	vivimos
viviste	vivisteis
vivió	vivieron

Special "yo" Forms in the Preterit

Some verbs in the preterit have special *yo* forms. We'll use the verbs *buscar, pagar,* and *empezar* as examples.

buscar – to look for

busqué	buscamos
buscaste	buscastais
buscó	buscaron

pagar – to pay

pagué	pagamos
pagaste	pagasteis
pagó	pagaron

empezar – to start, to begin

empecé	empezamos
empezaste	empezasteis
empezó	empezaron

These verbs have special *yo* forms to preserve the original sound of the consonant in the infinitive.

Sandal Verbs

In the present there are shoe verbs. In the preterit there are *sandal verbs*. I have also heard these called *he/they halfway verbs*, but I prefer to call them *sandal verbs*. Look at the following two verbs:

dormir – to sleep

dormí	dormimos
dormiste	dormisteis
durmió	**durmieron**

sentir – to feel

sentí	sentimos
sentiste	sentisteis
sintió	**sintieron**

Imagine a sandal drawn around the bolded forms of these verbs.

"Other" Verbs

I call these the *other* verbs because I can't think of a good name for them. There is a group of at least ten verbs that are considered irregular. But there is a pattern to them. They all have the same endings. Their stems are irregular.

Endings for these verbs:

e	imos
iste	isteis
o	ieron

Following is a list of verbs that follow this pattern along with their stems.

andar – anduv-
caber – cup-
estar – estuv-
haber – hub-
hacer – hic- (c changes to z in 3rd person)
poder – pud-
querer – quis-
saber – sup-
tener – tuv-
venir – vin-

Instead of learning these verbs as irregular, learn them as a group of verbs with a different set of endings.

"J" Ending Verbs

There is small group of verbs whose preterit stem ends in a j. These follow the same pattern as the *other* verbs, but the i in the 3rd person plural form drops.

decir – to say, to tell

dije	dijimos
dijiste	dijisteis
dijo	**dijeron**

conducir – to drive

conduje	condujimos
condujiste	condujisteis
condujo	**condujeron**

traducir – to translate

traduje	tradujimos
tradujiste	tradujisteis
tradujo	**tradujeron**

traer – to bring

traje	trajimos
trajiste	trajisteis
trajo	**trajeron**

Irregular Verbs

Now that we've examined the regular verbs, we can move on to the irregular verbs. But since we're considering most of the "irregular" verbs as regular verbs, we don't have very many left.

The verbs *ser, ir,* and *dar* are irregular. The preterit conjugation of *ser* and *ir* are exactly the same.

ser/ir – to be/to go

fui	fuimos
fuiste	fuisteis
fue	fueron

dar – to give

di	dimos
diste	disteis
dio	dieron

When to Use the Preterit

To learn the uses of the preterit, use the acronym **STARS**.

Sudden occurrence
Time limit/Completed Action
Action disrupts the action of the verb in the imperfect
Reaction to another action
Series of distinct instances

Examples of preterit:

Empezó a llover.
It started to rain.
(Sudden occurence, complete action)

Llovió por dos horas.
It rained for two hours.
(time limit)

Yo estudiaba cuando sonó el teléfono.
I was studying when the phone rang.
(action disrupts the action of imperfect verb)

Cuando mi hermano usó mis zapatos, me enojé.
When my brother wore my shoes, I got mad.
(reaction to another action)

Leí este libro dos veces.
I read this book twice.
(series of distinct instances)

To learn more about the uses of the imperfect and the preterit, consult *Demystifying Spanish Grammar*.

Present Perfect

The present perfect tense is formed by taking the present tense of the verb *haber* and adding the past participle of the main verb.

haber – to have

he	hemos
has	habéis
ha	han

Past Participles:

hablar – hablado
comer – comdio
vivir – vivido

(Some past participles are irregular.)

This tense is used to express actions that happened in the recent past. It corresponds to the English present perfect. Look at the following sentence:

Ya he hecho mi tarea.
I've already done my homework.

In Spain the present perfect is often used instead of the preterit. It sort of has the same function as the French *passé compose.*

Pluscuamperfecto (Pluperfect)

The *pluscuamperfecto* is a past tense to express what happened BEFORE another past action. It is formed by conjugating the verb *haber* in the imperfect tense and adding the past participle of the main verb.

haber – to have (imperfect)

había	habíamos
habías	habíais
había	habían

hablar – to speak (*pluscuamperfect*)

había hablado	habíamos hablado
habías hablado	habíais hablado
había hablado	habían hablado

Example:

Yo había hecho mi tarea cuando mi hermano llegó.
I had done my homework when my brother arrived.

The action of doing the homework happened before the brother arrived. Therefore, the *pluscuamperfecto* is used.

Translate the following sentences:

1. My mother had spoken to me before I left.

2. When my sister arrived, I had finished my homework.

3. When the students left class, the professor had taught them a lot.

Pretérito Anterior (Preterit Perfect)

The *pretérito anterior* is used for the same reasons as the *pluscuamperfecto*. The difference is that this tense isn't used anymore in modern Spanish. It is now reserved for literature. So you should still learn to recognize it. It is formed by conjugating *haber* in the preterit and adding the past participle of the main verb.

haber – to have (preterit)

hube	hubimos
hubiste	hubisteis
hubo	hubieron

hablar – to speak (*pretérito anterior*)

hube hablado	hubimos hablado
hubiste hablado	hubisteis hablado
hubo hablado	hubieron hablado

Other Past Tenses

The other past tenses that we'll look at are the imperfect progressive, the preterit progressive, and the immediate past.

The imperfect and preterit progressive tenses both require the verb *estar* in either the imperfect or the preterit with the present participle of the main verb. Read the following two sentences. There is a very subtle difference in the meaning.

Yo estaba leyendo un libro. – *I was reading a book.*

Yo estuve leyendo un libro. – *I was reading a book.*

They both translate into the same sentence in English, but there is a very subtle difference between them. The first sentence indicates that the speaker was reading a book without interruption. The second indicates that the speaker was reading a book with interruption. To avoid ambiguity one should add something to the second sentence like a time frame.

Yo estuve leyendo un libro hasta la medianoche.
I was reading a book until midnight.

If you add a time frame like *hasta la medianoche*, the preterit progressive is required. But you can avoid both of these tenses by using the imperfect. It will work in both cases.

hablar – to speak (imperfect progressive)

estaba hablando	estábamos hablando
estabas hablando	estabais hablando
estaba hablando	estaban hablando

hablar – to speak (preterit progressive)

estuve hablando	estuvimos hablando
estuviste hablando	estuvisteis hablando
estuvo hablando	estuvieron hablando

Immediate Past

The immediate past is formed with the present tense of the verb *acabar* + *de* + the infinitive of the main verb. It translates to "has just."

Example:

La profesora acaba de salir.
The professor has just left.

The imperfect of *acabar* + *de* + the infinitive of the main verb translates to "had just."

Example:

La profesora acababa de salir.
The professor had just left.

4 Future Tenses

As I stated earlier, the future tense in Spanish is not used as much as a future tense. Even though it is used as a future tense occasionally, it's being used more and more to convey probability.

Simple Future

Verbs in the simple future are always regular. The endings are the same for all of them. The only thing that can be irregular is the stem of the verbs.

hablar – to speak

hablaré	hablaremos
hablarás	hablaréis
hablará	hablarán

comer – to eat

comeré	comeremos
comerás	comeréis
comerá	comerán

vivir – to live

viviré	viviremos
vivirás	viviréis
vivirá	vivirán

Here's a list of verbs whose stem is irregular in the future tense. The same stem is also used for the conditional.

caber – cabr-
decir – dir-
haber – habr-
hacer – har-
poder – podr-
poner – pondr-
querer – querr-
saber – sabr-
salir – saldr-
tener – tendr-
valer – valdr-
venir – vendr-

Examples of future:

Lloverá mañana.
It will rain tomorrow. (future action)

Mi hermano estará en casa.
My brother is probably at home. (probability)

The simple future can be used to express future actions, but it's very common to use the future to convey probability. Most speakers would prefer to say

Va a llover mañana.

or even
Llueve mañana.

The present tense is often used in place of the future.

Future Perfect

The future perfect tense is used to express when one future action occurs before another future action. It is formed with the future tense of *haber* + the past participle of the main verb.

haber – to have

habré	habremos
habrás	habréis
habrá	habrán

Examples:

Yo habré aprendido español cuando me gradúe de la universidad.
I will have learned Spanish when I graduate from college.

Ella habrá terminado su cena cuando su hermano llegue.
She will have finished her dinner when her brother arrives.

Translate the following sentences:

1. I will have done my homework when my friend calls.

2. When I arrive at church, my sister will have already sung.

The "Fake" Future

The so-called "fake" future was explained in the chapter on the present tense.

Old Construction of "haber de + INFINITIVE"

When you read old Spanish literature, you will definitely come across the old way of constructing the future tense. It was originally formed by taking the present tense of *haber* + *de* + the infinitive of the main verb.

Example:
Yo he de hablar. – I will speak. (old way)
Yo hablaré. – I will speak. (modern way)

If you look closely, you'll see that the present forms of *haber* eventually became attached to the end of the infinitive.

hablar – to speak

hablar+he=hablaré	hablar+hemos=hablaremos
hablar+has=hablarás	hablar+habréis=hablaréis
hablar+ha=hablará	hablar+han=hablarán

5 Conditional Tense/Mood

Before we begin the chapter on the conditional, we need to establish whether it is a tense or a mood. Tense indicates time, whereas mood indicates the intention. Most would consider the conditional to be a mood since it expresses hypothetical situations, which has nothing to do with time. But I can see how the conditional can be described as a mood in some cases, but a verb tense in others. The conditional can be used to express a future action from a past point of view. Look at the following sentences:

No lo haría si yo fuera tú.
I wouldn't do that if I were you.
(Hypothetical situation: The conditional is being used as a mood in this sentence.)

Mi hermana me dijo que vendría a la fiesta.
My sister told me she would come to the party.
(Future action from past point of view)

The last sentence can easily be reworded to

Mi hermana me dijo, "Vendré a la fiesta."
My sister told me, "I'll come to the party."

Simple Conditional

The conditional is formed by taking the stem of the verb in the future tense and adding the appropriate endings.

tener – tendr

tendr*ía*	tendr*íamos*
tendr*ías*	tendr*íais*
tendr*ía*	tendr*ían*

The endings for the conditional are exactly the same as the endings for –er/-ir verbs in the imperfect.

Conditional Perfect

The conditional perfect is formed by taking the simple conditional of *haber* and adding the past participle of the main verb.

hablar

habr*ía* hablado	habr*íamos* hablado
habr*ías* hablado	habr*íais* hablado
habr*ía* hablado	habr*ían* hablado

The conditional perfect is used mostly as the result clause in conditional sentences. There are three main types of conditional sentences.

	"Si" clause	"Result" clause
1	Present Indicative	Simple Future
2	Imperfect Subjunctive	Simple Conditional
3	Past Perfect Subjunctive	Simple Conditional Perfect

The "si" clause ("if" clause in English) conveys a hypothetical situation. The result clause conveys what would be if the "si" clause were true.

Examples:

Si haces tu tarea, aprenderás más.
If you do your homework, you will learn more.
(present/future)

Si tuviera más dinero, iría a España.
If I had more money, I would go to Spain.
(imperfect subjunctive/conditional)

Si hubiera tenido más dinero, haría ido a España.
If I had had more money, I would've gone to Spain.
(past perfect subjunctive/conditional perfect)

6 The Subjunctive

The Spanish subjunctive is probably the most difficult thing that you will ever encounter in Spanish grammar. The subjunctive frustrates many students. It's easy to see why. It has so many uses and takes up nearly forty pages in John Butt's book *A New Reference Grammar of Modern Spanish.* I will explain the subjunctive the traditional way and my way. One thing that many students assume about the subjunctive is that it always conveys doubt. This is only one of the many uses.

Conjugating the subjunctive is relatively easy. Take the *yo* form of the present indicative, remove the -o, and add the appropriate endings. It is said that the verbs take "opposite" endings.

	sing. (-ar)	plural	sing. (-er)	plural	sing. (-ir)	plural
1	hable	hablemos	coma	comamos	viva	vivamos
2	hables	habléis	comas	comáis	vivas	viváis
3	hable	hablen	coma	coman	viva	vivan

There are six commonly used verbs that are irregular in the present subjunctive. You can remember them with the acronym DISHES.

Dar
Ir
Ser
Haber
Estar
Saber

	ser sing.	ser plural	estar sing.	estar plural	haber sing.	haber plural
1	sea	seamos	esté	estemos	haya	hayamos
2	seas	seáis	estés	estéis	hayas	hayáis
3	sea	sean	esté	estén	haya	hayan

	dar sing.	dar plural	ir sing.	ir plural	saber sing.	saber plural
1	dé	demos	vaya	vayamos	sepa	sepamos
2	des	deis	vayas	vayáis	sepas	sepáis
3	dé	den	vaya	vayan	sepa	sepan

*Some teachers prefer not to teach *dar* and *haber* when they begin to teach which verbs are irregular in the present subjunctive. If we remove these two verbs, we can use the following acronym: SEIS.

Ser
Estar
Ir
Saber

    The traditional method of teaching the subjunctive is to explain its uses in nominal clauses, adjective clauses, and adverbial clauses. These clauses are always dependent; therefore, there must also be an independent/main clause. In nominal and adjective clauses there must also be a change of subject from the independent clause to the independent clause.

Nominal clause- when the clause is the direct object of the verb of the main clause.

Example:
Quiero que vengas conmigo.

The direct object of *querer* is "que vengas conmigo." It is the nominal clause. There is also a change of subject from the independent clause to the dependent clause.

Adjective clause- when the clause modifies the direct object of the verb in the main clause.

Example:
Busco a alguien que hable francés.

The direct object *alguien* is being modified by the adjective clause "que hable francés."

Adverbial clause- when the clause modifies the verb of the main clause.

Example:
Puedes jugar cuando termines tu tarea.

The adverbial clause is "cuando termines tu tarea."

All this may sound like Greek to you, but don't worry. Other students feel the same way. I explain the subjunctive with the acronym DINNER. But this only applies to nominal and adjective clauses.

Doubt/uncertainty
Influence
Non-existence
Negating certain verbs
Emotional reactions
Required conjunctions
  A menos de que - unless
  Sino que – but rather that
  Para que - so that
  Antes de que - before
  Con tal que – provided that
  En caso de que - in case that

Examples of subjunctive

1. *Dudo que venga.*
   I doubt he is coming.
2. *No estamos seguros de que tengas razón.*
   We're not sure that you're right.
3. *Ella quiere que yo me vaya.*
   She wants me to go away.
4. *Mi madre me dice que limpie mi cuarto.*
   My mother tells me to clean my room.
5. *Me alegro de que estés aquí.*
   I'm glad you're here.
6. *Ellos temen que esté muerto su padre.*
   They fear that their father is dead.
7. *Siempre estudio a menos de que mi novia esté conmigo.*
   I always study unless my girlfriend is with me.
8. *Mis padres trabajan para que tengamos dinero.*
   My parents work so that we have money.

Imperfect Subjunctive

The imperfect subjunctive is used for the same reasons as the present subjunctive, but the verb in the main clause is in a past tense (usually the imperfect or the preterit tense).

The imperfect subjunctive is formed by taking the 3rd person plural form of the verb, removing the ending *-ron*, and adding the appropriate endings.

hablar
hablaron

	sing.	plural
1	habla*ra*	hablá*ramos*
2	habla*ras*	habla*rais*
3	habla*ra*	habla*ran*

These are called the -ra endings. There is another set of endings called the -se endings. They mean the same thing, but the -ra forms are used more in conversation. The -se endings are reserved for writing in most Spanish speaking countries. The -se endings are commonly used in conversation in Spain.

	sing.	plural
1	habla*se*	hablá*semos*
2	habla*ses*	habla*seis*
3	habla*se*	habla*sen*

Examples of Imperfect Subjunctive

Mi madre quería que yo limpiara mi cuarto.
My mother wanted me to clean my room.

No estábamos seguros de que vinieras.
We weren't sure that you were coming.

Tenía miedo de que mi perro estuviera muerto.
I was afraid that my dog was dead.

El profesor les dijo a sus estudiantes que hicieran su tarea.
The professor told his students to do their homework.

Ella quería ir al cine antes de que lloviera.
She wanted to go to the movies before it rained.

La estudiante le llamó a un tutor para que comprendiera mejor el subjuntivo.
The student called a tutor so that she might understand the subjunctive better.

Present Perfect Subjunctive

The present perfect subjunctive is used when the verb in the main clause is in the present indicative, but the action of the verb in the dependent clause occurs before the action of the main verb.

It is formed by taking the present subjunctive of the verb *haber* and adding the past participle of the verb.
Example:

Dudo que hayas hecho tu tarea.
I doubt that you have done your homework.

Dudar is in the present indicative, but the action of the verb *hacer* occurs before the action of the verb *dudar*. Look at the following sentence.

Dudo que hagas tu tarea.
I doubt that you are doing your homework.

Dudar is in the present indicative, and the action of *hacer* occurs at the same moment. Therefore, the present subjunctive is used.

haber (present subjunctive)

	Singular	Plural
1	haya	hayamos
2	hayas	hayáis
3	haya	hayan

Past Perfect Subjunctive

The past perfect subjunctive is used when the verb in the main clause is in a past tense, but the action of the verb in the dependent clause occurs before the action of the main verb.

It is formed by taking the imperfect subjunctive of the verb *haber* and adding the past participle of the verb.

Example

Dudé que hubiera hecho su tarea.
I doubted that he had done his homework.

Dudar is in the preterit tense, and the verb *hacer* is in the past perfect subjunctive because the action occurs before the action of the verb *dudar*.

Dudé que hiciera su tarea.
I doubted that he was doing his homework.

The action of the verbs *dudar* and *hacer* are simultaneous.

7 Other Possible Tenses

There are other possible tenses used in Spanish that haven't yet been explained in this book, and these tenses usually aren't explained in other books on Spanish grammar. I don't know of a particular name for these tenses, but I'll refer to them as the *perfect progressive* tenses. You've already learned all the possible perfect tenses. A *perfect progressive* tense is formed by taking a perfect tense of the verb *estar* and adding the present participle of the main verb. We do this in English all the time.

I have spoken. (present perfect)
I have been speaking. (present perfect progressive)

He hablado. (present perfect)
He estado hablando. (present perfect progressive)

The construction is

haber + *estado* + PRESENT PARTICIPLE

These tenses are used the same way they are in English. Instead of using the above construction, you can also use

llevar + PRESENT PARTICIPLE

Llevo hablando español por cinco años.
I have been speaking Spanish for five years.

You can also say

He estado hablando por cinco años.

Past Perfect Progressive

Había estado hablando.
Llevaba hablando.
I had been speaking.

Future Perfect Progressive

Habré estado hablando.
Llevaré hablando.
I will have been speaking.

Conditional Perfect Progressive

Habría estado hablando.
Llevaría hablando.
I would've been speaking.

Present Perfect Progressive Subjunctive

Es posible que haya estado hablando español toda su vida.
Es posible que lleve hablado español toda su vida.
It's possible that he's been speaking Spanish his whole life.

Past Perfect Progressive Subjunctive

*Era posible que había estado trabajando desde el
principio.*
*Era posible que llevaría trabajando desde el
principio.*
It was possible that he had been working along.

Even though these tenses are possible in
Spanish, they are not used as much as the perfect
tenses in English. And when these tenses are used,
the construction *llevar* + PRESENT PARTICIPLE
is more common.

8 More on Spanish Verbs

Now all we have left to look at are voice and other uses of *haber*. In Spanish there are active voice and passive voice, just as in English.

Active Voice vs. Passive Voice

The difference between active and passive voice is difficult to explain without examples. Read the following two sentences.

The dog bit John. (active)
John was bitten by the dog. (passive)

These sentences have the exact same meaning, but the first sentence is active, and the second is passive. The direct object of the active sentence becomes the subject of the passive sentence. The subject of the active voice becomes the agent (the agent has the word *by* before it). The active verb becomes passive with a form of the verb *to be* plus the past participle.

El perro murdió a Juan. (active)
Juan fue mordido por el perro. (passive)

In Spanish the passive voice is formed by taking a conjugate form of the verb *ser* and adding the past participle of the main verb. It is sometimes possible to use *estar*, but Spanish speakers would prefer to use the active voice whenever possible. The passive voice is too *weak*.

"There is/are"

Español	Inglés
hay	there is/are
*había	there was/were
*hubo	there was/were
habrá	there will be
habría	there would be
haya	(no equivalent)
hubiera/hubiese	(no equivalent)
debe haber	there must be
debería haber	there should be
necesita haber	there needs to be
va a haber	there is going to be
iba a haber	there was going to be

Examples:

Hay una silla.
There is a chair.

Hay dos sillas.
There are two chairs.

Había un accidente.
There was an accident.

Había dos coches.

There were two cars.

Hubo un accidente.
There was an accident.

Habrá un examen mañana.
There will be an exam tomorrow.

Habría más tiempo si el profesor no hubiera hablado tanto.
There would be more time if the professor hadn't talked so much.

No creo que haya bastante tiempo.
I don't think there's enough time.

No creía que hubiera bastante tiempo.
I didn't think there was enough time.

Debe haber un camino.
There must be away.

Debería haber dos cajeras los domingos.
There should be two cashiers on Sundays.

Necesita haber más esctructura en la clase.
There needs to be more structure in the class.

Va a haber una tormenta.
There is going to be a storm.

Creía que iba a haber bastante tiempo.
I thought there was going to be enough time.

*The imperfect is used to describe something, and the preterit is used when something happened all of a sudden.

No-Fault Construction

The no-fault construction is the other use of *se* I discussed earlier in the book. The no-fault construction is also called *el "se" accidental*. It is used with certain verbs when something unplanned happens. It's also used to remove the blame from someone. The most commonly used verbs that use *el "se" accidental* are

acabar
caer
ocurrir
olvidar
perder
quedar
romper

When using *el "se" accidental*, the most commonly used verb tense is the preterit.

Examples:

Se nos acabó _asoline.
We ran out of gas.

Se me cayeron los libros.
I dropped the books.

Examples of removing the blame:

Yo rompí la ventana.
I broke the window (on purpose).

Se me rompió la ventana.
I broke the window (by accident).

The no-fault construction is formed

se + IO pronoun + 3rd person verb form

The *se* is always required. The indirect object pronoun indicates the person to whom the unplanned event happened. The verb form is always in the 3rd person, which can be either singular or plural according to the direct object.

Expressing "Keeps on + INFINTIVE"

If you want to express *keeps on* + *INFINITIVE*, use the construction

seguir + PRESENT PARTICIPLE

Examples:

El niño siguió mirando la television.
The boy kept on watching TV.

Le duele la pierna, pero sigue jugando al fútbol.
Her leg hurts, but she keeps on playing soccer.

Expressing Verb + "away"

If you want to say a verb plus *away*, use the construction

irse + PRESENT PARTICIPLE of Main Verb

Examples:

El pájaro se fue volando.
The bird flew away.

Me fui corriendo.
I ran away.

The Infinitive

The infinitive form of the verb is the form you find in the dictionary. It always ends in –ar, -er, or –ir. Other than being the verb in "neutral gear," so to speak, it is also used as a verbal noun.

Fumar es malo para la salud.
Smoking is bad for your health.

In English we use the –ing form of the verb as a verbal noun. In Spanish we use the infinitive.

9 Conclusion

By now you should have a better understanding of Spanish verbs. Learning Spanish verbs can be very challenging, but the learning process can be simplified with the right materials. Hopefully, this book has simplified your learning of Spanish verbs.

Recommended Books on Spanish

501 Spanish Verbs
by Christopher Kendris

Barron's Spanish Verbs
by Christopher Kendris

Demystifying Spanish Grammar
by Brandon Simpson

Practice Makes Perfect: Spanish Verb Tenses
by Dorothy Richmond

Practice Makes Perfect: The Spanish Subjuncive Up-Close
by Eric Vogt

Practice Makes Perfect: Spanish Past Tenses Up Close
by Eric Vogt

Spanish Verbs for Dummies
by Cecie Kraynak

Spanish Verbs: Ser and Estar: Key to Mastering the Language
by Juan and Susan Serrano

Verb Chart

Verb _____ Tense _____

yo		nosotros	
tú		vosotros	
él/ella/usted		ellos/ellas/ ustedes	

Verb _____ Tense _____

yo		nosotros	
tú		vosotros	
él/ella/usted		ellos/ellas/ ustedes	

Verb _____ Tense _____

yo		nosotros	
tú		vosotros	
él/ella/usted		ellos/ellas/ ustedes	

84 | Brandon Simpson

Verb_____ Tense_____

yo		nosotros	
tú		vosotros	
él/ella/usted		ellos/ellas/ ustedes	

Verb_____ Tense_____

yo		nosotros	
tú		vosotros	
él/ella/usted		ellos/ellas/ ustedes	

Verb_____ Tense_____

yo		nosotros	
tú		vosotros	
él/ella/usted		ellos/ellas/ ustedes	

Lightning Source UK Ltd.
Milton Keynes UK
UKOW052230300413

210005UK00001B/167/P